CHURCH INBREED

WHEN THE CHURCH DATES THE WORLD

In a world of uncertainty and demoralizing values, the church has adopted the world in its operations creating Inbred Christians.

By
Sylvia Copeland-Murphy
Chesapeake, Virginia

Editors
Brenda C. Brown
Dr. William S. Hampton
Rev. Ronda King Smith

Cover design
Kimberly Austin

CHURCH INBREED
Sylvia Copeland-Murphy

Published by:
SCM VISION
P.O. Box 16253
Chesapeake, VA 23328-6253
1-855-SCM-VIZN

ISBN 978-0-9838895-0-2
LCCN: 2011913787

Printed in the United States by Morris Publishing®
3212 East Highway 30
Kearney, NE 68847
1-800-650-7888

Table of Contents

Acknowledgements

I give praise and honor to the Triune God for inspiring, guiding, and empowering me through the completion of this work! Much appreciation is given to my Pastor, Dr. Anthony Copeland and his wife for their spiritual support. When the obstacles seemed insurmountable, my husband Thurman was my coach, pushing me to the finish line. A great amount of motivation came from my sons, AJ and Ronald who were always encouraging and edging me on, thanks! Certainly, I thank my mother, sisters, and brothers for their prayers, wisdom, and faith in me. Special thanks to my three editors and cover designer who gave doctrinal, grammatical, and constructive criticism, which made this effort possible. Thanks to everyone who scattered and planted seeds in my life resulting in this blessed harvest.

INTRODUCTION

Church Inbreed foretells when the church dates the world and reveals the fleshliness of believers that hinders their maturity in Christ. Despite their divisive spirits and human reasoning, their attitudes are symptomatic of their carnality. God has ordained the release of this book at such a time when spiritual resources are plentiful but godly relationships are few. The term "Inbred Christian", used repeatedly, describes the action and behavior of believers who attend church and proclaim Salvation in Christ, yet holding on to the world. They depict traits of the carnal minded and continue to serve the flesh. The carnal mind is enmity against God and is not subject to the Law of God.

The motivation for writing this book about the church dating the world derived from an influx of ungodly qualities among church people. It is puzzling and saddening to see so many believers willfully sin without godly repentance. The church used to be a place where one went for moral and spiritual support. Today, it is world accommodating: overflowing with proud and stiff neck believers serving as leaders before a Holy God. Believers seem to have completely given themselves over to idolatry and have failed to worship the true and living God. This collapse of holiness and sanctification originated from interbreeding pleasure-oriented worship with pure and authentic service.

During a time of wrong conduct in the church, it is befitting for Christians to denounce the clever and unbiblical teachings of the Word of God. For the purpose of this book, an "Inbred Christian" is people deceived by Satan who professes Christianity, yet not follow it as a rule of life. To make a distinction between the Born Again Christian and the carnal person, the term "Inbred Christian" is used.

Church Inbreed reveals a prototype of religious behaviors and activities that emulate Christianity. It conveys a spiritual image of Salvation by people of the Christian faith, but is a deception of Satan. The difference between *Inbred Christians* and *Born Again Christians* is the foundation upon which they build their faith. If Christians build their faith upon any foundation other than Jesus Christ, they are inbred. An Inbred Christian is a faithful member of a local assembly committed to ministry, man, positions, and titles with a form of godliness. A Born Again Christian is a faithful servant of Jesus Christ who received his new creation to serve God in His will, way, and word. As declared in the Scriptures, the heart changes in Salvation, to glorify God not to return back to sin.

Throughout the course of this book, illustrations of Inbred Christians occur because of the vulnerable actions of the church appeasing the world. The definition of an Inbred Christian eliminates the possibility of the reader thinking a person that is born again can lose their Salvation. In no way can a Born Again Christian lose his Salvation because of the redeeming blood of Jesus Christ. The interchangeable usage of the word "Christian" transpires in the book to acknowledge the faith of the person.

The truth of the matter is when man does not receive Christ in his heart, he lacks the opportunity of Salvation; living as an Inbred Christian. Within a congregational setting, Inbred Christians intermingle with Born Again Christians. Because this blending is repeatedly subtle, no church is exempt from this epidemic.

Overlooking improper behavior in Houses of Worship does not resolve the quandary of inbreeding, rather escalates it out of control.

The inception of Church Inbreed is the manifestation of worldly attributes replaced with substitutes for divine truth. Church Inbreed is most prevalent in churches where there is a blending of the world and religion. The significance of Bible doctrine exposes false teachings and provides instructions for a clean and practical way of living. A continual practice of religious and worldly engagements results in an unregenerate people. The term regeneration means new birth or born again therefore, unregenerate means not born again. In these end times, Pastors are guilty of walking away from their congregations, churches have become padlocked due to division and strife, and persons boldly proclaim Salvation without the convictions of God's Word through the Holy Spirit.

Church Inbreed is a compelling book to read! You as the reader will have to ponder within yourself, "Am I serving, living for, and obeying man or God?" Church Inbreed points to three things: the knowledge of sin "*By the Law"*; the continuance of sin *"Under the Law"*; and the defeat of sin *"Above the Law"*. Church Inbreed will bring resolution to the warring soul, redemption to the dying soul, and Salvation to the lost soul.

Chapter 1
By the Law

"By the law is the knowledge of sin".
Romans 3:20

No Longer By the Law

Romans 3:20, "Therefore by the deeds of the law there shall no flesh be justified in his sight: for by the law is the knowledge of sin."

Confused, disturbed, frustrated, unworthy, failure, undisciplined, and carnally minded are characteristics of Inbred Christians trying to live by the Law. They struggle with the challenges to do right, the misunderstanding of faith, and the will to please God. The deception and manipulation of Satan has thrust these believers from Christ and caused their hearts to revert to their old ways. It is pertinent that Christians realize the difference between living by the Law and living by faith in God. As long as men live by the Law, the Law has dominion over him. The Law is unable to keep him from sinning and cannot forgive him for his sins. The Law confines, restricts, and accuses. When a Christian lives by the Law, he lives in guilt, shame, and condemnation. Romans 7:1 states: "the law hath dominion over a man as long as he liveth; (2) For the woman which hath an husband is bound by the law to her husband so long as he liveth."

Moreover, *Grace* removes the *rule of the Law* and dominates man as long as he has accepted Jesus Christ as his personal Savior. In no way does, this passage provides the believer with an excuse to end his or her marriage. However, because Inbred Christians often function out of religiosity in lieu of a solid relationship with Christ, their marriages are more likely to suffer greatly with issues of infidelity and deception. Inbred Christians serve man, therefore he or she is more obsessed with self-image than Salvation. A Born Again Christian may choose to endure an abusive marriage, not because he/she is so in love with the spouse, but because of the vow in God's covenant of marriage. A Christian marriage symbolizes the relationship between Jesus Christ and His Church. Therefore, the true believer should hold his marriage in high regard as a sacred covenant between spouse, God the Father, God the Son, and God the Holy Spirit. Satan deceives couples to live *by the Law* instead of by the Grace of God because God's grace allows for forgiveness and reconciliation. This deception creates an atmosphere of uncertainty, imbalance, compromising, and pseudo worship that contributes to Church Inbreed. Until

Inbred Christians totally surrender their lives to the will of God, the Law binds them. It is by faith in Jesus Christ that Born Again Christians live and not by the Law.

Man is free from the bondage of sin when he accepts Jesus Christ. The blood cleanses the heart and instead of living by the Law, the heart lives by the Word of God. Instead of struggling with the Law, the Christian lives above the Law in Grace. Love uncovers sin, forgives sin, erases sin, and washes away sin. Jesus Christ fulfilled the Law and now the Holy Spirit guides the life of the believer. Romans 10:4, "For Christ is the end of the law for righteousness to everyone that believeth".

These end times have ushered in Church Inbreed and launched the church into dating the world. A paradigm shift of doctrinal Christian foundation emerged in the last three decades of the 20th Century. As Pastors began to perform their ministerial roles in a full time capacity, seminary became popular to secure an occupation, but not with the indwelling of the Holy Spirit. The custom now is that church pulpit search committees seek Pastors based upon their level of education, and agility in pulpit antics and vocal theatrics. Ironically, this is where the *"religious divide"* invaded churches.

Some men and women of the cloth have manipulated seminary as an instrument for a source of income and not as a method for winning souls. While Christian Education is essential for survival according to the Word of God, its intention is not for abuse or misuse of filthy lucre. It is commanded in II Timothy 2:15, "Study to show thyself approved unto God, a workman that needeth not to be ashamed, rightly dividing the word of truth". Most assuredly, Pastors need to know and live by the Word of God because the Holy Scriptures mandate that to be so. God's Word also teaches that the lack of knowledge leads to the destruction of Christians. According to Hosea Chapter 4, this chapter demonstrates the impending results of rejecting the knowledge of God, "...My people are destroyed for lack of knowledge: because thou has rejected knowledge, I will also reject thee, that thou shalt be no priest to me: seeing thou has forgotten the law of thy God, I will also forget thy children".

Congregants need to elect Pastors based upon God's Word and not titles behind their names. As cited in

Hosea 4:6, "My people are destroyed for lack of knowledge". This is not *Seminary* purely *Commentary*. Humanity often refuses to take God's Word and apply it to every aspect of their lives, including the church. The knowledge that the Word of God offers is not effective when Christians decline to live by it. Therefore, the continuous rejection of God's Word and knowledge of Him is a consequence of God's rejection of man. In addition, Hosea maintains, "that thou shalt be no priest to me: seeing that thou hast forgotten the law of thy God". This emphatically calls out those in leadership roles serving as Pastors, Preachers, Priests, Elders, Prelates, Bishops, Cardinals, Apostles, Evangelists, etc. God said, "Thou shalt be no priest to me". Church Inbreed is a result of churches removing the Law of God from their foundation: The Ten Commandments, the Beatitudes, the Lord's Prayers, and yes, even the 66 Books of the Bible. In summary, to make the Law of God pronounced, humanity must decide to live by God's Holy Word.

Beginning with leadership, man has removed and rejected God's Word and organized the church as the world. It is with great urgency that the Triune God (God the Father, God the Son, God the Holy Spirit) be brought back into the church. Visibly and spiritually, there ought to be a distinct difference between the world's standards and practices and the standards and practices of the church. Hosea 4:7 continues with "And there shall be, like people, like priest: and I will punish them for their ways, and reward them their doings." Selecting Pastors that will please the people is a common practice of today's churches. God never established Pastors to charm the people. He ordained Pastors to lead His people in accordance with His Word, thus pleasing Him. When the church is guilty of catering to the wants of the world, rather than ministering to the needs of the carnal minded it results in Church Inbreed. Furthermore, church pulpits are not platforms for gain and self-promotion; God will punish and reward this type of behavior in accordance with Hosea 4:9.

Many churches have removed God's Law from their assemblies, and replaced them with "By-Laws". By-Laws are the fundamental structure of an Organization, Board, or Council. These rules set a standard, which governs the people as they operate the organizations' mission and vision on a daily basis. By-Laws are set to accommodate the organization and keep order, fairness, equality, and justice among its members. The problems with By-Laws are that: (1) Man sets them, and therefore is subject to change at any time for convenience sake. The Law of God never changes; (2) By-Laws are the basic structure of an organization. God created His church as an Organism; a living, active and productive body; and (3) By-Laws exist within a Democratic environment; governed by the people. The design of God's church was not to function as a Democracy: rather a Theocracy governed by Sovereign God.

The Church In The Wilderness

Acts 7:38, "This is he, that was in the church in the wilderness with the angel which spake to him in the mount Sīʹna, and with our fathers: who received the lively oracles to give unto us: (39) To whom our fathers would not obey, but thrust him from them, and in their hearts turned back again into Egypt."

In this 21st Century, the church is perceived as the congregation of modern day Israelites wandering in the wilderness. Although Moses had prophesied Jesus Christ, the Israelites hearts were still towards Egypt. Similarly, the church today, with its' charismatic flair, preaches Jesus Christ but has much conformity to the world. Through disobedience, man has promoted idol worship and has forced away Jesus from among them. An idol according to the dictionary is "an object of excessive devotion or admiration". Question: To whom or what has humanity devoted life? To regard anything as a substitute for Jesus Christ is to make that thing a god. The first commandment quoted in Exodus 20:3 is "Thou shalt have no other gods before me". The object that distracts man from Jesus and lures him to excessive devotion to the flesh, eventually becomes his god. That which is being admired more than Jesus Christ brings about disobedience in the body of

Christ. The church in the wilderness is as the soul in misery. Quite often, more confusion, hatred, disobedience, and lust culminate among people within the church. A man wrestles with his soul before fighting with others. Consumption of immoral living brings misery to the soul and robs a Christian of a meaningful and abundant life in the Spirit.

Consider a person that is miserable in a situation verses a person that is miserable in their soul. A circumstance that makes one miserable can change with a modified lifestyle choice, only God can transform the person suffering with misery of the soul. When there is vexation of the soul, the believer lives in the wilderness. Eventually, a person operating in this agony will self-destruct and bring damnation to his soul. The recourse that occurred with the children in the wilderness was not a result of Moses going up on Mount Sinai but from the souls' heart condition. The foundational principle needed to discourage a child of God from going back to his old ways is the principle of the heart. It is a known fact that before the actual act of backsliding is committed, the heart desires it. The Old Testament Proverbs forewarns

Christians to guard one's heart and the New Testament commands that he puts on the armor of God. What a person believes in his heart is what he becomes.

It is by the Law that the knowledge of sin comes as mentioned in Romans 3:20. Ignorance and deception have blinded the eyes of believers living by the Law. There is not a law on the face of this earth that can free man from sin. A man recognizes and uncovers sin by the Law however; it does not liberate him from sin. Furthermore, a man's sin convicts him by the Law but is unable to convert him. The Law can uncover a man's guilt before a just God yet, God is the only lawgiver who can save and destroy. If there were no law, man would not know that sin exists. Because the Law is a guide to live by, Christians hide behind the Law to appear righteous. According to God's Word, the Law is not for the righteous. Just men keep the Law. It does not make them righteous but simply a "Law Keeper". There are many "Law Keepers" leading the church in the wilderness and causing souls to remain lost.

A "Law Keeper" is an individual who has no relationship with Jesus Christ, notwithstanding, he observes and keeps the Law of Moses. A "Law Keeper" believes in abiding by the letter instead of living in the Spirit. According to, II Corinthians 3:6, "...for the letter killeth, but the spirit giveth life". Paul compares the Law with the Spirit of Christ and concludes that the only thing the "Law Keeper" does is condemn each other with the Law and kill their witness by the Law. "Law Keepers" are void of life, love, emotion, and power. Church Inbreed inadvertently manifests in congregations due to leaders who are "Law Keepers" and are not Spirit-filled. When an attitude of a leader is above the Law, it disrupts matters of the heart. The Law of Moses and the Word of God serves two distinct purposes.

THE LAW OF MOSES	THE WORD OF GOD
Punishes	Forgives
Convicts	Converts
Exposes	Disposes
Kills	Lives
Bounds	Sets Free

One must realize that the Law does not justify man before God. Since the Law is unable to make man righteous before God, the whole world stands in need of something more than the Mosaic Law. If it had not been for the Law, man would not have an awareness of sin. The

Pauline Epistle of Romans 7:7 says, "What shall we say then? Is the law sin? God forbid. Nay, I had not known sin, but by the law: for I had not known lust, except the law had said, Thou shalt not covet." The function of the Law awakens man's consciousness towards sin. When the Law reveals sin, the normalcy of man is to abide by the Law to avoid sinning. It is man's nature to sin. There are laws in every aspect of life wherein all people must abide. Therefore, people practice how to obey laws more so than how to obey and please Jesus.

The Wilderness of Sin

Exodus 17:1, "And all the congregation of the children of Israel journeyed from the wilderness of Sin, after their journeys, according to the commandment of the Lord, and pitched in Rephidim: and there was no water for the people to drink."

The Lord, the righteous God delivers man out of all his sin. It is man who wanders back into the wilderness of sin. God does not deliver man to bring him back again to bondage! The Wilderness of Sin is the satisfaction of the flesh. When the Israelites were in Egypt, referred to as the Church in the Wilderness, they did not understand their destiny. They had physically journeyed out of Egypt, nevertheless experienced mental bondage. Man provides for the flesh, God provides for the Spirit. The Israelites were dissatisfied with the conditions of their journey and began to complain against Moses. So often in life, Born Again Christians become displeased with this Christian journey and begin to murmur and complain. They look back at Egypt, fail to trust God, and become consumed with their past. Egypt represents a past life of sin. When sin measures sin with sin and compares sin by sin, the outcome is always sin. Going back to a life of sin only benefits the flesh. Similarly, it deprives the Christian and keeps him in the wilderness of sin.

Believers face a related dilemma just as the Israelites in their journey from this wilderness experience. Living holy requires leaving Egypt (a life of sin) and submitting to Christ. When the church dates the world, the Christian has a crossbreed of church/world relationship. Typically, this hybridization results in enslavement and spiritual exhaustion. Situations that burden and bind the believer are not God-ordained. Man was not born to carry burdens, pain, hurt, guilt, and pride. The human body's design is to praise the Lord and cast everything upon Jesus.

Christians leave Egypt but they fail to change kings. Enslavement to a "Pharaoh King" challenges the believer before, during, and after transitioning. Even though Christians want deliverance from spiritual bondage, they trade off God for Pharaoh. Satan's deception caused the Israelites to believe that going back to Egypt was better than being with the Lord. Born Again Christians fall but they do not go back. However, Inbred Christians go back. Fear causes them to go back! Doubt causes them to go back! A lack of faith causes them to go back! This occurs frequently because Inbred Christians fail to develop and establish a personal relationship with their new King through praying, studying, meditating, and reading God's Word. Man's expectation of the new King (Jesus Christ) will be that of the last king if he has not acquainted himself with the new Kings' plan and   promises.

Redemption did not come in the form of a slave but rather through the act of freedom. Just as God heard the groaning of the Israelites in Egypt, He hears believers today. The Lord God is immutable and regardless of the obstacles in the wilderness, there is an escape route for the believer.

The Wilderness of the Red Sea

Exodus 4:21, "And the Lord said unto Moses, when thou goest to return into Egypt, see that thou do all those   wonders before Pharaoh, which I have put in thine hand: but I will harden his heart, that he shall not let the people go".

Serving the wrong king can result in a life of excessive drama; a pattern of inconsistency; a journey to nowhere; and a willingness to be a slave. Satan's M.O. (Mode of Operation) is not to let God's people go. The children of Israel were halt between two opinions: to follow Moses or go back to Egypt. Pharaoh's heart was hardened which made the journey difficult. The mission of Satan is to disrupt the Christian's journey, making it difficult, with frustrating, humiliating, and challenging circumstances. He uses Christians against Christians, driving a wedge between them and Christ, and producing a harden heart.

A man's heart is harden when he fails to obey God as written in Matthew 19:8, "He saith unto them, Moses because of the hardness of your hearts suffered you to put away your wives: but from the beginning it was not so." The enemy escalates the divorce rate among Christian marriages because of the hardening of the hearts. Christian divorcing is a contentious topic that leaves the believer with confusing and unrequited questions. Oftentimes, the joining of two in marriage may be with Inbred Christians unaware of their new creation as defined in II Corinthians 5:17. A lack of or absence of reading God's Word warrants a harden heart. Church attendance alone cannot bring about conversion in the hearts of man. Consequently, when one fails to meditate on God's Word, he begins to follow man and his own mind. The results are deadly leaving the soul exposed to the enemy as prey.

The Savior, Satan, and Self are three voices (thoughts) that speak to Christians daily, not necessarily in that order. So many Christians cannot differentiate the Savior's voice from Self or Satan. Jesus speaks to the heart of a person because the heart is spiritual; Self and Satan speak to the mind because the mind is fleshly. Whenever the heart is stimulated to serve in love edifying another, it is of the Savior. If a voice (thought) to serve comes to mind for recognition, promotion, status, or self-gain; that is of Self. When a voice speaks to the mind that rationalizes, negotiates, and compromises that which is good; that is of Satan. Whenever God is out of the reckoning, there is no one left but Satan and Self. The study of God's Word causes man to use the Word as a *"weapon of choice"*. Weaponry, when used properly under the leading of Holy Spirit, destroys false doctrines, disbands false prophets, and dissolves false teachings. In Paul's Epistle of Romans 7:18, he shares "For I know that in me (that is, in my flesh) dwelleth no good thing: for to will is present with me; but how to perform that which is good I find not". When good thoughts enter the mind, the Holy Spirit places them there by speaking to the heart of man. Satan and/or Self speak to man's heart by tainting pure thoughts with motives other than to serve Christ.

Chapter 2
Under the Law

"Now we know that what things soever the law saith, it saith to them who are under the law."
Romans 3:19

The Vicious Cycle

Genesis 6:5-8, "And God saw that the wickedness of man was great in the earth, and that every imagination of the thoughts of his heart was only evil continually. (6) And it repented the Lord that he made man on the earth, and it grieved him at his heart. (7) And the Lord said, I will destroy man whom I have created from the face of the earth; both man, and beast, and the creeping thing, and the fowls of the air; for it repenteth me that I have made them. (8) But Noah found grace in the eyes of the Lord."

It is amazing how the vicious cycle of the wickedness of man plays out in the Bible, in the church, in society, and in the lives of humanity. From the time span of creation to the introduction of Noah, God was grieved that he made man. At one time or another, it has grieved a mother or father that a child was born. A child full of anger, animosity, strife, rebellion, foolishness, and sin can grieve a parent. Man relentlessly repeats history, yields to temptation, and gives way to an unpredictable heart. Nothing that man attempts to do is new. It is a new generation, but the cycle is still vicious. As quoted in Ecclesiastes 1:9, "The thing that hath been, it is that which shall be; and that which is done is that which shall be done: and there is no new thing under the sun". As Born Again Christians, one may want to do an extraordinary work to prove his love towards Christ, yet there is nothing

31

new under the sun. The one and only thing that is worth completing in this "vicious cycle" called life is to serve the Lord thy God and to be a servant of the Gospel of Jesus Christ. This may not grant one a lasting reputation, but it will give him access to eternal life. Acquiring name, fame, promotion, position, and status release spirits that prompt pride, ego, power and an attitude. These spirits multiply and dominate from generation to generation evolving into the wickedness of man.

Regardless of Salvation through Christ, people continue to murder, divorce, steal, hate, lie, commit adultery, fornicate, and the list goes on. The wickedness of man still exists even with the building of mega churches, the outreach of community engagement, and the reviving of the saints. Contrary to what man might believe, Born Again Christians still sin. Therefore, sin subsists through-out the basements of churches, within the confinements of seminary, around the temples of the diocese, and in the hearts of some believers. It is true that Jesus Christ died for the sins of man still men find themselves sinning. The Word of God does not condone sins; in contrast, provides an Advocate if man happens to sin. I John 2:1, "My little children, these things write I unto you, that ye sin not. And if any man sin, we have an advocate with the Father, Jesus Christ the Righteous: (2) And he is the propitiation for our sins: and not for ours only, but also for the sins of the whole world".

God already knows that Born Again Christians will sin. Even so, He has placed Jesus Christ in position to advocate on their behalf. Why do Christians need an advocate? Jesus serves as Advocate because He pleads man's cause before Almighty God. When man sins, he leaves the will of God and enters the enemy's showground. Once in the enemy's showground, Satan begins accusing the believer before God.

God is the only one who can allow the enemy access to His children. Therefore, man needs someone to advocate when Satan goes before God accusing him of sin. If Jesus died while men were yet sinners, be it not strange that He would plead their cases as believers. In Revelation 12:10, it states: "And I heard a loud voice saying in heaven, now is come salvation, and strength, and the kingdom of our God, and the power of his Christ: for the accuser of our brethren is cast down, which accused them before our God day and night". Satan accuses believers before God day and night proposing to gain control and power over them. This is why it is important to strive and stay in the will of God; and equally important to acknowledge one's sin and ask God's forgiveness. In Heaven, Christ advocates when He hears a repentant heart and moves on behalf of the believer. It does not hurt anyone to repent nevertheless it harms every believer who does not repent.

Humanity still behaves in the manner as the people in Noah's days with unbelief: living in oblivion with no loyalty to Christ. It is expedient that man captures God's attention with his faith and service. Otherwise, he is bound for destruction. Of all the wickedness found in the world, "Noah found grace in the eyes of the Lord". Noah's lifestyle broke the "vicious cycle" of wickedness, which spared him and his family from destruction. Noah was the advocate for God pleading with the people that it was going to rain. The people rejected him, refused to listen, and made a mockery out of his redundant sermon. On the other hand, the church and world have become obstinate to the message "Jesus is coming back". The wickedness of man's heart remains; even with sermons preached globally that Jesus is soon to return. Man has become so creative in trying to win souls that churches are beginning to resemble the world. Just because some things are popular does not mean that it makes the soul prosperous. Moreover, rather than feeding the Spirit, the flesh is being fed operating as a conduit for Church Inbreed. Although Noah's message was unpopular, he kept preaching for the saving of souls.

There are millions advocating and crusading for Christ, but the masses have chosen to travel the broad way to destruction. The Lord promises never to destroy the earth with rain again howbeit the next time by fire. I John 2:2 recites, "Jesus is the propitiation for our sins: and not for ours only, but also for the sins of the whole world". Jesus restores good will by the washing away of sins with His blood. All humanity though wicked, has the same opportunity for Salvation.

Hew Down the Tree

Daniel 4:20 states: "The tree that thou sawest, which grew, and was strong, whose height reached unto the heaven, and the sight thereof to all the earth; (21) whose leaves were fair, and the fruit thereof much, and in it was meat for all; under which the beasts of the field dwelt, and upon whose branches the fowls of the heaven had their habitation: (22) It is thou, O king, that art grown and become strong: for thy greatness is grown, and reacheth unto heaven, and thy dominion to the end of the earth. (23) And whereas the king saw a watcher and an holy one coming down from heaven, and saying, Hew the tree down, and destroy it; yet leave the stump of the roots thereof in the earth, even with a band of iron and brass, in the tender grass of the field; and let it be wet with the dew of heaven, and let his portion be with the beasts of the field, till seven times pass over him."

The King Nebuchadnezzar symbolizes church leadership that suffers from Church Inbreed. As powerful as Nebuchadnezzar was, God invaded his life with a reality check that resulted in a loss of wealth, health, and power. Leadership that misuses the Word of God for self-gain is offensive to the mission of Christ and an obstruction of Christianity. It is time for true believers to declare truth with controversy making unbelievers uncomfortable in the presence and places of God. The spiritual definition of compromise for the believer means to negotiate God's truths and live as an undercover agent with an apprehensive heart. Compromising God's Word erupts from a carnal mind and creates an environment of hybridize Christians. A heart that is intimidated compromises God's Word. The antidote Christians need to impede Church Inbreed is to declare the Gospel of Jesus Christ with a controversial, yet, compelling message that the wages of sin is still death. God does not promote controversy that divides solely controversy that edifies and set free.

II Timothy 3:1 says "This know also that in the last days perilous times shall come". Lamentably, that time has come where the church and the world desire the same lustful fulfillments. The new modern day churches have infrastructures that are technologically sound, youth-friendly, world accommodating, and lack consistent praise, prayer, and worship. This movement admonishes doctrinal teachings and caters to "tailored made ministries" inclusive of all needs. Although change is sometimes inevitable, God is still immutable. The difficulty with churches that are world accommodating is that the congregants face challenges such as building their faith on a spiritual foundation or secular one. A faithful servant is one that emphasizes subordination to God and executes his faithfulness through integrity and commitment. Today, it is almost impossible to differentiate the saved from the unsaved with gospel music resembling R & B, and the true worshippers from the liars with their rejection of the infallible revelation of God for godly wisdom. It is no wonder souls are still in bondage and converts are still perverts, because churches have adopted an all-inclusive salvation.

Social networking has destroyed personal relationships and caused young people to struggle with their identity, let alone their relationships with Christ. The sacredness of holy living and holy worship has faded away and new converts come into God's presence with gadgets, gimmicks, and "gods". Breaking this mode of religiosity brings into question the authenticity of the new birth. There is a desperate cry for churches to go back to basic Christian instructions and stop appealing to the masses with worldly tactics.

Another one of Satan's tactics is to disrupt and dissolve the plan of God for the Christians' life. When Spiritual Leaders, lift self instead of Jesus, destruction invades the Kingdom of God. Before God's people are lost, God will *"hew down the tree"*. In this story with King Nebuchadnezzar, God demonstrated to this leader and reminded him that, *"the Most High ruleth in the kingdom of men, and giveth it to whomsoever he will, and setteth up over it the basest of men"*. Due to the crossbreed of church and world, Spiritual Leaders rule through Pride, Ego, Power, and Attitude (PEPA). The transition of PEPA leadership is when God changes a leaders' heart from man and let a beast's heart indwell him. PEPA leadership becomes obsessed with the blessed things of God and abruptly rules with self-gratifying motives.

The "get rich scheme" among religious leaders is prosperity preaching that is void of preaching for soul Salvation. The United States should not have a crisis with low-income, at-risk youth, or domestic violence with all its' mega-churches and mega-ministries. When Spiritual Leaders fail to obey God, the consequences are unmistakably earth shattering and mind boggling. The Scripture text concludes: *"Whose leaves were fair, and the fruit thereof much, and in it was meat for all; (the Word of God) under which the beasts of the field dwelt, and upon whose branches the fowls of the   heaven had their habitation (the whole creation)"*. At this point, Daniel interpreted the dream as speaking about Nebuchadnezzar when he says, *"this is you*

O'King". This too is symbolic of Spiritual Leaders who have grown and become strong. *"For thy greatness is grown, and reacheth unto heaven, and thy dominion to the end of the earth. And whereas the king saw a watcher and an holy one coming down from heaven, and saying, "Hew the tree down, and destroy it, yet leave the stump of the roots thereof in the earth"*.

The message here is to cut the leader down and destroy him, however leave his soul intact because God will one day restore him. This is God's Kingdom and when leaders become like Nebuchadnezzar, He will hew down the tree. This case in point reflects television evangelists, church-wide officers, and common spiritual authority in localized communities. Even though God uses the basest of man, He wants man to remain abased and not exalt himself above Him. As men think more highly of themselves than they ought, destruction invades their kingdoms. Romans 12:3 states: *"For I say, through the grace given unto me, to every man that is among you, not to think, of himself more highly than he ought to think; but to think soberly, according as God hath dealt to every man the measure of faith"*.

The making of a King Nebuchadnezzar begins when Spiritual Leaders become compromising and not controversial. Compromise keeps down tension, keeps the people satisfied, and keeps the money coming. Controversy threatens position, disrupts authority, and questions financial stability. Leaders have mastered compromise to resemble holiness that abides peaceably by the Word of God. **Warning:** This sacrilegious practice results in exile and detachment from the privileges and blessings of God. Compromising does not represent Christ but Judas Iscariot, King Saul, and Satan. However, those that ignited controversy stood on God's Word which resulted in an exile on the isle of Patmos (John); a stoning to death (Stephen); an ex-communication (Paul); an imprisonment and decapitation (John the Baptist); and yes, even a crucifixion (Jesus).

To compromise God's Word is to live under the Law as an unbeliever. To compromise is to waiver in the faith that God is not who He says He is. To compromise is to put self over Salvation and jeopardize the souls God has provided. When the church dates the world, games become the trend. The game of "Jeopardy" is when crossbred Pastors jeopardize their relationships with God for seasons of pleasure and wealth. Double Jeopardy is, when they use God's Word for "income" and not the Spiritual "outcome". It is unfortunate that leaders mimic each other, having acquired appetites for a "Wheel of Fortune"; modeling church organization and structure like the world rather than after God. If every biblical character were David, then Ezekiel's bones would not have come together; God would have silenced Job's testimony; and Noah could have disobeyed and not built the ark. Not all Pastors and/or Preachers may win a "Wheel of Fortune", but all must win souls. Instead of soul winning, some Pastors negotiate into the game of "Let's Make a Deal". The deal Satan makes with these Spiritual Leaders is to rid the service of the sanctity of praise and worship: to attract and entice people with his entertainment and sideshows. By using this technique, churches become mesmerized with choreographic movements, in-sync clapping, swaying, and foot stomping beats while suspending the rudiments of true worship and getting in the presence of a Holy God.

Nothing can be more of a detriment than Pastors who serve because "The Price Is Right". What does it profit a man to gain the whole world and lose his own soul? Pastors of Church Inbreed have led congregations to a spiritual drought, left with unsatisfied appetites for the Word. Ever willing to do what is good but never finding the knowledge to accomplish it. Entertainment does not bring deliverance from strongholds, spiritual defeat, and bondage. During two-hours of church worship, people experience a "spiritual high" that fades shortly after the benediction and leaves them literally fighting for their lives. It is symbolic to a person on a respirator; instead of breathing on his own, the machine does it for him. Instead of living on the Word of God, the entertainment does it for them. Therefore, just like the respirator, when the patient comes off, he dies. When the entertainment stops, the spirit dies.

This type of environment creates a breeding ground for corruption and places a price tag on the lives of the believers. To create an atmosphere of teaching, discipline, and meditation would render unappealing and boring.

Even so, church order needs a spiritual developmental process that operates God's way and not man's way.

Lip Salvation

Matthew 15:7-9, "Ye hypocrites, well did Esaias prophesy of you saying, (8) This people draweth nigh unto me with their mouth, and honoureth me with their lips; but their heart is far from me. (9) But in vain they do worship me, teaching for doctrines the commandments of men."

Church Inbreed is where Spiritual Leaders teach for doctrines the commandments of men, which are principles that lack consequences or the price one pays that willfully sin. This doctrine excludes terminology such as sin, hell, Satan, and anything that suggests there is the wrath of God. As unspiritual as it may sound, lip salvation is how Satan has deceived many in believing their salvation is valid. This is not a popular topic for discussion but a needed one for conversion. So many have come to the altar on a moment of remorse, with a sorrowful emotion, or a pitiful heart and confessed Salvation however never received Jesus in their hearts. Romans 10:8, "But what saith it? The word is nigh thee, even in thy mouth, and in thy heart: that is, the word of faith, which we preach". Inbred Christians casually confess the Word nevertheless fail to live by it. Moreover, the Word is yet in the Inbred Christian's mouth, still it has a difficult time finding habitation in the heart. If the Word of God has not taken root in the heart of a man, then Salvation is only voiced and not exercised. The soul converts when the heart receives the Word, considering that the seat of conviction is in the heart, and preaching the Gospel persuades man's heart towards change.

All the same, the preached Word makes one conscious of his own sin, when the Holy Spirit pricks the heart unto Salvation. If man has only stated Salvation from his lips, can the Word of God convict his lips? The heart must be the habitat for Christ so that Spirit of Truth can arrest the soul. Otherwise, the soul is lost and without a Savior. The Scripture proceeds in Romans "That if thou shalt confess with thy mouth the Lord Jesus, and shalt believe in thine heart that God hath raised him from the dead, thou shalt be saved". This is the area where Inbred Christians become complacent and rest their Salvation on their lips, because this kind of belief requires action.

If Salvation only involved believing, then Jesus did not have to come and die on the cross. Man could have just believed in Him and He could have stayed in Heaven and never experienced the agony of the cross. This specific type of belief, (1) Commands trust in Jesus and not man;

(2) Commands self-denial; and (3) Commands living by the precepts of Christ; and the Gospel. At this junction of Salvation, belief in the heart alters the way a person lives, forgives, and dies. If Christ lives in the heart, forgiveness is not an option. It is impossible for man to live righteously without Jesus abiding in his heart.

A lip salvation satisfies flesh, perpetrates a fraud, and pleases man. A lip salvation is stagnating in the faith, influenced by the world, and defiant to Christ. Lip salvation is untraceable, imperceptible, and barely discernible in a church that dates the world. The word hypocrite describes this group of people, which are lukewarm, neither hot nor cold. As Church Inbreed evolves, worship becomes a formality wherein Inbred Christians fail to fear God in their hearts. There is so much self-indulgence in places of worship that the Word of God is minimized and personal agendas maximized. Ministry should reach the needs of the people. The number of people present on Sunday morning should not be the tool used to measure church growth; rather the converted heart. A church driven by self-indulgence will not and cannot survive on the commandments of men as doctrinal teaching. To persist in this way, creates vain worship and desensitizes man's spirit to the things of Christ.

In the Old Testament scriptures, Isaiah 29:13 says, "Wherefore the Lord said, forasmuch as this people draw near me with their mouth, and with their lips do honour me, but have removed their heart far from me, and their fear toward me is taught by the precept of men". The precept of men is the acceptance and behavior of man over a Righteous and Holy God. Ironically, Isaiah prophesied this message, Paul testified it, and Church Inbreed legalized it.

A Spirit of Deep Sleep

Isaiah 29:10-12, "For the Lord hath poured out upon you the Spirit of deep sleep, and hath closed your eyes: the prophets and your rulers, the seers hath he covered. (11) And the vision of all is become unto you as the words of a book that is sealed, which men deliver to one that is learned, saying, Read this, I pray thee: and he saith, I cannot; for it is sealed: (12) And the book is delivered to him that is not learned, saying, Read this, I pray thee: and he saith, I am not learned."

What a powerful and profound message delivered to Judah by the prophet Isaiah. The spirit of deep sleep hovers over congregations that only expect messages that are hopeful, helpful, and harmless. It is good to give hope to the hopeless but even better to emphasize the integrity of God's Word. If Spiritual Leaders never preach a message of correction or reproof, one could interpret that God does not punish sin. In Isaiah's description of the Lord, pouring out a spirit of deep sleep represents a lack of Biblical teaching or no teaching at all. A great number of congregations are ignorant of true spiritual principles and attend church as a form of tradition and/or formality. This overflow of church attendance, with the learned as well as the unlearned, does not convey a need to meditate on the Word of God. With all that lies within, man must read and meditate on God's Word in order to work out his own Salvation through fear and trembling. Paying tithes,

49

attending a two-hour worship experience, and serving in a ministry does not validate that the person knows God.

If a man chooses not to read the Bible, he goes about his day living according to the precepts of man and not the promises of God. A man that lives according to his own beliefs is a covenant breaker and falls under the Law instead of in the grace of God. Because people do not read God's Word, they live out of His will and fall prey to the snares and traps of the enemy. Reading the Word of God allows a person to apply the Scriptures to his/her life. Millions accept Jesus Christ as their Savior, and still live a miserable Christian life. Unaware of God's promises, purpose, and plans for their lives, they become victims of their own self-righteousness. These Inbred Christians read everything from daily devotionals to life enrichment books; attend yearly conferences and retreats coupled with leadership trainings that provide minimal joy and a spirit of heaviness instead of a garment of praise.

This defeating spirit leaves them embarrassed and ashamed reluctant to reveal the truth about their inner warfare. To add insult to injury, this is not just church lay members but Spiritual Leaders as well. Isaiah said the spirit poured out was a deep sleep that closed the eyes of the prophets, the rulers, and the seers. A sleeping leader is one that refuses to acknowledge God in his teachings with whom God has turned over to a reprobate. As recorded in II Timothy 3:7-9, "Ever learning, and never able to come to the knowledge of the truth. (8) Now as Jannes and Jambres withstood Moses, so do these also resist the truth: men of corrupt minds reprobate concerning the faith. (9) But they shall proceed no further; for their folly shall be manifest unto all men, as theirs also was". Reprobates have no potential for gain. They will become extinct leaving their followers scattered and unfulfilled. The spirit of reprobate is as prevalent today as was in Biblical times due to the educational background and inexhaustible credentials of Spiritual Leaders. Unfortunately, people are highly educated yet not in love with God. As quoted, "the Bible is occupied in millions of homes, but is the least read book in the world". Even though it has a remedy for every problem known to man, no one has mastered its' usage to eradicate man's problems.

The Royal Law

James 2:8-11: "If ye fulfill the royal law according to the scripture, thou shalt love thy neighbors as thyself, ye do well: (9) But if ye have respect to persons, ye commit sin, and are convinced of the law as transgressors. (10) For whosoever shall keep the whole law, and yet offend in one point, he is guilty of all. (11) For he that said, Do not commit adultery, said also, Do not kill. Now if thou commit no adultery, yet if thou kill, thou art become a transgressor of the law."

In essence, the royal law is symbolic of kingship and/or represents royalty. This particular law when fulfilled has rank above every existing law before humanity. Royal is an adjective that describes a kingdom and its government; "suitable for a king or queen; magnificent; Stately, and regal". The Scripture translates that whoever fulfills the royal law has the characteristic of the King. To live as a Born Again Christian, a person must be Christ-like and portray Christ's character. A Christian's life should emulate the Creator and exhibit conduct reflecting the priesthood. When this is not the case, it is because Church Inbreed exists and leadership eviscerates sound doctrinal truth. Church Inbreed is a direct indication that the heart has a malfunction and cannot effectively fulfill God's commandments. The keyword in the royal law is "love". In John 3:16 it states: "For God so loved the world" which illustrates not only God's feelings

52

for the world, but His actions towards it that "He gave His only begotten son". A Christian must feel love for others as well as show love. God gave up what was lovable for the unlovable; the sinless for the sinful; and the glory for the shame. A Christian must love when it is not popular to love. He must love when love is unreciprocated: in times of persecution and rejection. Fulfillment of the royal law is to "love your enemies, bless them that curse you, do good to them that hate you, and pray for them which despitefully use you, and persecute you".

The royal law will give the Born Again Christian a prayer to pray for his enemy that causes his enemy to be at peace with him. When man fulfills the royal law, God will give him a tongue that speaks those things that are not as though they were. When man fulfills the royal law, he receives restoration, recovery takes place, and revival is come. The royal law nailed sin to a cross, took captivity captive, and left Satan powerless. Man has all power to fulfill the royal law but relinquishes it to the enemy. In order to dismiss the spirit that breeds respect of persons, one must practice discipline and love. Trials and tribulation coupled with wicked and unloving people invade the lives of believers to perfect the royal law. The only way to love those that offend is to be offended; those that hate is to be hated; and those that discriminate is to be discriminated against.

The Lord allows circumstances to impact a believer's life for spiritual employment, characteristic enhancement, and royal endowment. The Spirit of Christ fulfills the believer with God's love, which enables him to walk after the Spirit to avoid fulfilling the flesh's lust. Galatians 5:14-16 states: "For all the law is fulfilled in one word, even in this; Thou shalt love thy neighbor as thyself. (15) But if ye bite and devour one another, take heed that ye be not consumed one of another. (16) This I say then, Walk in the Spirit, and ye shall not fulfill the lust of the flesh". The Spirit of Christ keeps the believer rooted and grounded in love. Christians must employ love that allows them to serve and be servants. As long as the Spirit leads, the Born Again Christian is not under the law. Galatians 5:18, "But if ye be led of the Spirit, ye are not under the law".

The definition of a Born Again Christian is to be Christ-like and exude behavior that obeys and walks in the will, way, and word of God. The mandate is that every Born Again Christian fulfills the royal law, which is love. A Christian that does not love does not possess the characteristics of Christ. Accordingly, I Corinthians 13:4-7, "Charity suffereth long, and is kind; charity envieth not; charity vaunteth not itself, is not puffed up. (5) Doth not behave itself unseemly: seeketh not her own, is not easily provoked, thinketh no evil. (6) Rejoiceth not in iniquity, but rejoiceth in the truth; (7) Beareth all things, believeth all things, hopeth all things, endureth all things". This is the instrument needed to measure a Christian's love for Christ. Failure to measure up to these characteristics is reason enough to reexamine one's love.

The Christian's life is only meaningful when it is able to fulfill the royal law. Royal endowment provides the Christian with gifts, talents, abilities, wealth, promotion, skills, and a mind to engineer all his efforts to soul winning. When the most important issue is the eternal abode of a human soul, the royal law supersedes life itself. The outreach and mission of Christians have taken a downward spiral that lacks the power to transform lives. On the other hand, the endowment of the Holy

Spirit produces an anointing that empowers, encourages, and enlightens the soul. In order for this endowment to take place, one must first awaken to the Spirit of Christ. Jesus knocks at the door of the believers' heart but the believer has elected to occupy his agenda with personal ambitions. It is time for persons to allow Jesus in their hearts and stop living for self-gratification. An end to Church Inbreed must take place and true believers must take a stand for the cause of Christ. Discipline is a directive for every believer and if left unpracticed, it will wreak havoc in the dating of the church and the world. The world cannot abide in the church and imbue it's' principles and beliefs. Neither can the church witness to the world without the holiness and righteousness of God.

Chapter 3
"God's Grace"
Above the Law

"For sin shall not have dominion over you: for ye are not under the law, but under Grace."
Romans 6:14

Put On Jesus

Romans 13:12-14, "The night is far spent, the day is at hand: let us therefore cast off the works of darkness, and let us put on the armour of light. (13) Let us walk honestly, as in the day; not in rioting and drunkenness, not in chambering and wantonness, not in strife and envying. (14) But put ye on the Lord Jesus Christ, and make not provision for the flesh, to fulfill the lusts thereof".

To live above the Law, a Christian must put on the Lord Jesus Christ. No longer can believers use Romans 3:23 as a crutch to continue to sin. Man's innovative style of sugar coating the Gospel has catapulted into the church and world courtship. This method of modern day preaching has removed the sacredness of righteous living from Christian principles. To distinguish between the righteous and unrighteous is almost impossible because Inbred Christians have adopted multiple standards for "Christian Living". Churches have made Christianity so comfortable that a man's pleasure determines where he worships rather than whom he serves. The creation of Church Inbreed is unquestionably destructive to the human soul. Most accept this courtship as an act of accepting change and advancing the Kingdom of God. Instead of rebuking behaviors and conduct that promote Inbred Christians, personal feelings become more important than a persons' soul. According to Proverbs 27:5, "Open rebuke is better than secret love". Rebuke means to blame or scold in a sharp way; or to reprimand". No one likes rebuke. Rebuke hurts, reveals, exposes, discloses, uncovers, and makes known.

Satan's first deception with Church Inbreed is sowing a spirit of discord and confusion that invades the atmosphere when open rebuke is exercised against unending and unrighteous living. Satan uses this underhand method as a way to silence the voice of God and ultimately replace the rebuke with acceptance. Instead of Born Again Christians reconciling their differences, tension prevails and the offended, oftentimes Inbred Christians, develop attitudes instead of appreciation for someone showing them the error of their ways. Open rebuke, when seasoned with grace, is welcomed by Born Again Christians. They understand that the Scriptures declare that man confesses his faults one to another, and pray one for another, that spiritual healing might transpire. Nevertheless, the feelings of an Inbred Christian become exaggerated and the need for deliverance vanishes. The attention shifts from spiritual correction to personal emotions, which distracts the Christians and plants disunity.

Jesus openly rebuked sin and took the suffering of the cross to justify the sin debt. Jesus' sacrificial love displayed publicly rebuked the betrayal of Judas and the legalism of the Pharisees. To live above the Law, Christians must put on Jesus and practice open rebuke of blatant sin. They must take heed to what is divine and what is worldly. When a person engages in the divine nature of God, he escapes the corruption of this world. It does not mean the Born Again Christian is divine but it does mean that the Holy Spirit lives inside him.

II Peter 1:5-7 says, "And beside this, giving all diligence, add to your faith virtue; and to virtue knowledge; and to knowledge temperance; and to temperance patience; and to patience godliness; and to godliness brotherly kindness; and to brotherly kindness charity". To avoid exempting Jesus in the expression of Church Inbreed, Christians must add His divine nature to their faith resulting in correct doctrine for living. It proceeds to add goodness to the Christian's faith, which causes him to desire to do well. The only way a believer in

Christ knows good from evil is to know what the Word of God says. The study of God's Word allows goodness to add to knowledge, which divides the Word of Truth. When a Christian stumbles, conviction fills the heart and correct doctrine makes him return to his first love, Jesus the Christ.

It is sin to a Christian when he knows to do right and chooses not to. Therefore, to knowledge one must add temperance (self-control). Just because an individual knows, what the Word of God says does not mean he does what it says. Self-control is the act of giving reverence to God so that one's attitude might please Him. It is evident that self-control deflates egos; crucifies flesh; and destroys a haughty spirit. The key reason why Christians do not practice temperance (self-control) is because the old man chooses not to die. In accordance to John 12:24, "Except a corn of wheat fall into the ground and die, it abideth alone: but if it dies, it bringeth forth much fruit. He that loves his life shall lose it; and he that hateth his life in this world shall keep it unto life eternal".

A Den of Thieves

Matthew 21:12-13, "And Jesus went into the temple of God, and cast out all them that sold and bought in the temple, and overthrew the tables of the money changers, and the seats of them that sold doves, (13) And said unto them, It is written, my house shall be called the house of prayer: but ye have made it a den of thieves".

The second deception Satan uses as the church dates the world is the attack on Inbred Christians by perplexing their Salvation with secret sins. Instead of being transparent for godliness, they become proud and shameful. What an oxymoron. These Christians become proud by masking their sins in fear of being exposed. This deception creates an environment that is swollen with pride, competitiveness, inferiority, and a give and take mentality. Although shame is the ultimate driving force behind their actions, a conquering spirit of greed overwhelms them. They continuously live in defeat as long as they are highly esteemed in the eyes of man. Where there is no discipline, there is no discipleship.

In a world of spiritual shifts and mega ministries, dens of thieves have erupted with best practice, evidence-base churches cropping up globally. It works; it draws the people; it grows the church; and it pays the bills. To measure the outcome of best practices for church structure with business principles is to wipe out biblical truth. The Bible is the best practice that all churches should use as their model for the permanence of church worship, which eliminates church and world dating.

An evolution of corrupt worship extends out of the uniting of the world and church. Church Inbreed has unequivocally construed the mission of Christians as well as the role of the church. The danger of interbreeding sacred things of God with corrupt things of the world is that it nullifies the meaning of Jesus' death. An indiscriminate mixture of spiritual living with carnal living produces a crossbreed of worshippers. This plethora of worshippers floodgate churches and sends an ethical message of approval. Not only is this unethical but immoral. Galatians 2:21 states: "I do not frustrate the grace of God: for if righteousness comes by the law, then Christ is dead in vain".

There is an inoculation of world-ism, an annihilation of doctrinism, and activation of liberalism. Now is the time for Christians to reclaim territory (Houses of Worship) and take back the holy things of God. As the church dates the world, moral relativism substitutes as doctrine, which makes no effect of the Gospel of Christ. God is displeased with dens erected by men for worship with propaganda for souls. This unethical move is sweeping the world producing religious fissions and best practices for church growth. Worshippers today mistake working in the church as Salvation; failing to realize that Christ has completed everything needed for eternity.

The church must live by the grace of God. Born Again Christians live in the flesh but not by the flesh, yet by faith. The Apostle Paul penned in Galatians 2:20, "I am crucified with Christ: nevertheless I live; yet not I, but Christ liveth in me: and the life which I now live in the flesh I live by the faith of the Son of God, who loved me, and gave himself for me". So many believers fail to experience fully, the crucified life. Wherein, this new life enables the Christian to die unto the Law as a means of obtaining the righteousness of God. The crucified life can proclaim: (1) I have given up the world; (2) I am crucified with Christ; (3) I have died to the old man; and (4) I am resurrected as a new man. When love abides in the heart, the undertakings of Church Inbreed dissolve. This meltdown becomes apparent only through sanctification and obedience to Christ.

Church is where the most difficult and sensitive people gather as a place of refuge and restoration. Understanding how to deal with varying spirits challenges the Born Again Christian yet on the other hand, builds character and oftentimes teaches him patience. Spiritual Leaders must be watchful that the enemy does not use their sanctuaries as a breeding ground to disrupt the worship environment and exhaust the efficacy of the Holy Spirit. Jesus sent the Holy Spirit to comfort, guide, instruct, teach, and bring all things back to the Christians' memory. Yet, Church Inbreed produces a sacrilegious Inbred Christian that negatively affects the development of true and holy worship.

To avoid this interbreeding, there must be a consistent and steady teaching of Bible doctrine with practical living that impedes Church Inbreed. Living above the Law means to live according to the grace of God. Grace is who Jesus is and in fundamental nature, who man becomes. Because grace is "a sense of what is right and proper", man's obedience and trust in God makes known

God's grace in his life. Paul testifies to this in II Corinthians 9:8, "And God is able to make all grace abound toward you; that ye, always having all sufficiency in all things, may abound to every good work".

Dead to the Law

Galatians 2:18-19, "For if I build again the things which I destroyed, I make myself a transgressor. (19) For I through the law am dead to the law, that I might live unto God".

The third deception Satan uses with Church Inbreed is the manipulation against Inbred Christians having them justify their sins while remaining there. A person who no longer walks in darkness may sin but he does not live in sin. The purpose of Jesus' death was to destroy the works of the devil and bring Salvation to the lost. The crucifixion did not abolish the Law but the Law forewarns Christians that sin still exists. To "live in sin" and to "happen to sin" are very different. I John 2:1 states: "My little children, these things write I unto you, that ye sin not. And if any man sin, we have an advocate with the Father, Jesus Christ the righteous (2) And he is the propitiation for our sins: and not for ours only, but also for the sins of the whole world". When man dies to the Law, his spirit lives in Christ--above the Law (Grace).

Therefore, Christians need to utilize their Advocate who sits at the right hand of the Father. An advocate in the Scripture is a Spiritual Attorney for the Christian. The cost he pays for this attorney is priceless. It is a three-step process wherein: (1) He confesses sin; (2) He asks for forgiveness; and (3) He repents from the sin.   Unlike a Secular Attorney that receives money, the Spiritual Attorney (Jesus) accepts the above acts as payment for case dismissal. Christians disregard this act of mercy and commit sins habitually, expecting forgiveness. The Secular Attorney can be   expensive for adjudication, which makes a person apprehensive to repeat their offence. Then again, a continuance in sin is a much more dangerous and expensive undertaking, costing eternal damnation for souls. Man tramples over God's mercy and develops an attitude of servant/master role reversal.   Instead of man serving Jesus, he expects Jesus to serve him.

When the world sees no spiritual development (self-control, discipline) in the life of Christians, they proceed to date the church. Inbred Christians today have an abundant life of sexual immorality, hardened hearts, wanton love, lying tongues, and other worldly attributes. These behaviors are open invitations to connect with the world and live in sin expecting the Advocate to plead their cases. Once the enemy beguiles this Inbred Christian, he ensnares him   with   strongholds   and   deceives   him repeatedly. This role reversal has contaminated church worship to the point that man is seduced by leadership rather than having an interest in "Son-ship". Inbred Christian leadership is so conspicuous that congregants proclaim assignments from God as a means to elevate self.

The glamour of church leadership is a fourth deception Satan uses to date the church. Things that attract so many people to church leadership roles are the accolades one receives, the potential for wealth one obtains, and the popularity/publicity attached to the role. Even when Inbred Christians know they do not produce the Holy ways of God, they maintain their status as pompous leaders in the church. They are comfortable with their pretentious lifestyles and have no convictions in serving and leading the lost to Christ. This paints the picture of the blind leading the blind and both falling in the ditch. The ditches of Church Inbreed are growing deeper and wider vacuuming in all that are not rooted in the faith. These aspired leaders fail to realize that the blood of these same souls is on their hands. It is the responsibility of church leadership to warn the wicked and lost souls with the error of their ways. Ezekiel 3:17-19 states: "Son of man, I have made thee a watchman unto the house of Israel: therefore hear the word at my mouth, and give them warning from me. (18) When I say unto the wicked, Thou shalt surely die; and thou givest him not warning, nor speakest to warn the wicked from his wicked way, to save his life; the same wicked man shall die in his iniquity; but his blood will I require at thine hand. (19) Yet if thou warn the wicked and he turn not from his wickedness, nor from his wicked way, he shall die in his iniquity; but thou hast delivered thy soul".

Instead of prohibiting the world from acquiring leadership roles in the church, Spiritual Leaders use to justify their actions with the statement: "who are they to judge". By definition, to judge is to criticize man for his action not when his action rebels against the righteousness of God. There are relationships in the church that are devilish and serve as the foundation of inbreeding the church and world. If Jesus came to destroy the works of the devil (which he did), to live in sin characterizes devilish relationships. I John3:8-9 says, "He that committeth sin is of the devil; for the devil sinneth from the beginning. For this purpose, the son of God was manifested, that he might destroy the works of the devil. (9) Whosover is born of God doth not commit sin; for his seed remaineth in him: and he cannot sin, because he is born of God."

Some congregants, who are Inbred Christians, live a double lifestyle and cannot please the Lord. Christian conversion is not to live haphazardly and abuse the mercies of God. Jesus' death on the cross validates man's justification to salvation and gives him free access to the righteous judge. Old Testament Law could not save, but grace allows man to plead his case before the Son of God. Jesus sits on the right hand of the Father making intercession for man and justifying cases before a righteous judge. Lawful cases must go through judicial processes, secure a jury, and have an assigned attorney. However, being that man is dead to the Law and alive with Christ; Jesus pleads man's case and sets him free. Grace only can wipe away sins. Only grace can provide new mercies. Lamentations 3:21-23 says, "This I recall to my mind, therefore have I hope. (22) It is of the Lord's mercies that we are not consumed, because his compassions fail not. (23) They are new every morning: great is thy faithfulness". Without grace, man would be hopeless--that is why Jeremiah penned that God's mercy keeps man from consumption. It is evident that there is no shortage of sin and sin has never experienced a recession.

Church Inbreed has created a generation of vipers. As described in an earlier chapter, many Inbred Christians have only attained Salvation with their lips but failed to receive Jesus in their hearts. When the heart is void of Jesus, it produces bad fruit. When the world considers their righteousness by the Law and the church manipulates their Salvation above the Law this creates a mongrel. This indiscriminate blend looks holy, sounds holy, acts holy, and believes they are holy. Most would think it is holiness but as recorded in the book of Matthew 12:33-34: "Either make the tree good, and his fruit good; or else make the tree corrupt, and his fruit corrupt: for the tree is known by his fruit. (34) O generation of vipers, how can ye, being evil, speak good things? For out of the abundance of the heart the mouth speaketh". This crossbreed of Inbred Christians and the world produces a generation of vipers lacking good fruit. Until man loves

God with his whole heart, he will love the world and the things of this world.

Once a person becomes born again, he must not continue loving the world. The first step a Christian takes to overcome Church Inbreed is to let go of the world. It is spiritually impossible for a child of God to love the world and love the Lord too. It is a deception of the enemy when a Christian thinks he can love the world and the Lord, and live a born again life. He is actually an Inbred Christian, which is disreputable to the body of Christ. In I John 2:15-17, "Love not the world, neither the things that are in the world. If any man loves the world, the love of the Father is not in him. (16) For all that is in the world, the lust of the flesh, and the lust of the eyes, and the pride of life, is not of the Father, but is of the world. (17) And the world passeth away, and the lust thereof: but he that doeth the will of God abideth for ever."

"Lust of the eyes", is to satisfy one's appetite by what he sees with the visible eye. Instead of viewing things that are invisible, these persons view things in the natural, as would the world. This is due to a lack of reading God's Word, disobedience, and self-indulgence. Man begins to

lust for what he sees which is   opposite of faith and trusting in God. Unfortunately, this creates a lack of faith in God and without faith, it is impossible to please Him.

"Lust of the flesh", is to satisfy one's desire in the body by submitting to the flesh. The flesh then controls the persons' behavior, decisions, and motives. Unfortunately, the flesh does not know how to perform that which is good because nothing good dwells in it. When man allows the flesh to control his actions, his Spirit becomes captive, which deprives him of serving Christ. With the mind, man must serve the Law of God to be righteous otherwise; he serves the law of sin with his flesh.

"Pride of life", is to think more highly of oneself that ultimately leads to destruction. Man exalts himself above the knowledge of Christ when he becomes proud. This produces an attitude that holds him captive and makes him void of humility. Pride goes before destruction and a haughty spirit before a fall in accordance with Proverbs 16:18. The Lord does not set up His servants to fall, pride does.

Inbred Christians believe their salvation is of God because of titles and positions held in the church. Satan uses this delusion to confuse them and stir up strife with true believers that are firm in their faith. This conflict intensifies Church Inbreed and interrupts the deliverance of strongholds and breakthroughs. The world cannot operate the church and blatantly imbue their principles with the Commandments of God. Born Again Christians must embrace the vicarious death of Jesus and live righteously.

The Conscious Law

Romans 2:13-15, "For not the hearers of the law are just before God, but the doers of the law shall be justified. (14) For when the Gentiles, which have not the law, do by nature the things contained in the law, these, having not the law, are a law unto themselves: (15) which shew the work of the law written in their hearts, their conscious also bearing witness, and their thoughts the mean while accusing or else excusing one another".

Church Inbreed occurs when Pastors allow the world to have just as much, if not more, authority as God's ordained believers. Theoretically, it is humanly impossible to separate worldly people from true believers in the church. However, it is possible to let true believers lead the church as bona fide witnesses before a lost world. The Bible describes that the "hearers" of the Law are not just before God and the "doers" are the true believers whom God justifies. What good is the Law if man does not keep it and provide excuses for breaking it? A "hearer" does not receive the Gospel of Jesus Christ and therefore, is unable to live according to the Word of God. He is an Inbred Christian. On the contrary, a "doer" receives with meekness the engrafted Word, which is able to save his soul. He is a Born Again Christian. The "doer" is not simply satisfied with attending church but fulfillment in the royal law according to scripture wherein, "Thou shalt love thy neighbor as thyself". Social status and church positions motivate the "hearer". When man loves man as he loves himself, everything becomes Christ-driven and Christ-centered. The behaviors of the "hearers" and the "doers" become distinct and obvious.

Until Jesus is brought back to the believers' reckoning, Church Inbreed will escalate and spread like a wildfire. An analogy of Church Inbreed is a balloon full of helium rising to the sky with no direction but taken whichever way the wind blows. People have acquired an appetite for helium and desire to rise with power, authority, and position. The church now operates as everything but what God designed for it. There should be two separate organizations but the one known as "church" should not change its mission or comingle activities with the world. Church should still be the place where Jesus lives!

The framework for soul salvation must always be doctrine driven and not polluted with "political correctness" and worldly influence. Inside these organizational structures are two designs known as "The Church" and "The Outreach". The Church's mission is foundation base wherein the Outreach mission is business base. Both have a spiritual influence and mission for the saving of lost souls. In this time of apostasy, a church Inbred Christian is the fulfillment of Bible prophecy. The man of sin (Satan) sometimes mentioned as Anti-Christ has deceived and confused millions with anthropocentric missions as Biblical truths. Nevertheless, the entire contents of the Bible from Genesis to Revelation are Bible doctrinal principles for all Christians. Overall, it is a requirement for Christians to live Holy and Righteous through obedience to Christ, towards God. Instead of missions with a spiritual outreach for Salvation, fabricated missions have corrupted believers to work for Salvation. The reality is that "The Church" and "The Outreach" are of God and should work in tandem to fulfill the Great Commission. It is difficult to detect the "hearers" from the "doers" and the "doers" from the "hearers". Outreach is to get the lost in the church and the Church is to keep souls rooted in the faith.

II Thessalonians 2:4 says, "Who opposeth and exalteth himself above all that is called God, or that is worshipped; so that he as God sitteth in the temple of God, shewing himself that he is God". This one Scripture demonstrates the birthing of Church Inbreed and its' foundational existence. Church leaders play a critical role in the Kingdom of God and are responsible for feeding and nurturing souls. Satan seizes the church and dominates the order of service through worldly influence and infiltration. His entrance is so cunning that his presence has the misrepresentation as truth. Today's church leaders are exalted and highly esteemed with self-appointed positions. This type of leadership has grown wealthy and prosperous due to the injustice and extortion of Church Inbreed. In order to maintain positions and possessions, leaders avoid offending congregants with biblical truth that discloses sins' consequences, hell's reality, and Satan's existence. The world sits comfortably in the church without any type of conviction for their sins because of the removal of God's wrath from the sermons. Education does not qualify one to become a teacher or leader of the Gospel, but Christ qualifies an individual through the washing of the blood.

Since "The Church" and "The Outreach" have prospered, many are deceived that this is of God. Only true believers will stand and lose the profit to gain Christ. Most have it backwards wherein they lose Christ, to gain a profit. It is critical for the church to regain its' rightful place and allow God to reign in order to dissolve this church and world courtship. A continuation of Scripture from II Thessalonians 2:10-12 denotes "And with all deceivableness of unrighteousness in them that perish; because they received not the love of the truth, that they might be saved. (11) And for this cause God shall send them strong delusion, that they should believe a lie. (12) That they all might be damned who believed not the truth, but had pleasure in unrighteousness". Man is conscious of what is wrong nevertheless has fallen prey to greed and pride that impede corrective actions. The Word of God explicitly states that man perishes when he does not receive the truth. A "hearer" only hears the Word but a "doer" hears and does the will of the Father. Church Inbreed demonstrates how believers and unbelievers alike, comingle holy and unholy things because of their sinful pleasures. This is not acceptable by God and all will be damned that practice such unrighteousness.

True believers must learn to move away from their emotions, which are triggers that culminate into the lust of the flesh, the lust of the eyes, and the pride of life. They must learn to discipline themselves by the Word of God and walk after holiness. God's Word is not to be waivered or taken likely. It is a practiced principle, a sacred discourse, and a conveyed message through a spiritual pipeline for church development. In these end times, churches are embracing luxurious style of entertainment Christianity that showcases celebrity preaching, personalized ministries, and mega edifices. To separate this church and world hybrid, the difference between the two is necessary for remediation.

The Remedy for The Remnant

Romans 11:1-5, "I say then, Hath God cast away his people? God forbid. For I also am an Israelite, of the seed of Abraham, of the tribe of Benjamin. (2) God has not cast away his people which he foreknew. Wot ye not what the scripture saith of Elias? How he maketh intercession to God against Israel, saying, (3) Lord, they have killed thy prophets, and digged down thine altars; and I am left alone, and they seek my life. (4) But what saith the answer of God unto him? I have reserved to myself seven thousand men, who have not bowed the knee to the image of Baal. (5) Even so, then at this present time also there is a remnant according to the election of grace".

Even though Christians today have conflicting views that result in many beliefs, God still has a remnant seeking His righteousness. Healthy outreach for church development must be God-driven and God-centered. Outreach by design should be the footprint of Ephesians 4:11-12. The sole purpose behind outreach ministry is that gifted ministers win souls through the manifestation of God's Grace. God gives men spiritual gifts for use in multiple capacities that magnetically pull lost souls to the church. Outreach opens doors of opportunities that anointed men and women of God might serve others with the power of God. When the church serves as the foundation of outreach, this perfects the saint. The Outreach is specifically "A Means to an End" and The Church is "An End to a Means".

{A MEANS TO AN END}
"THE OUTREACH"

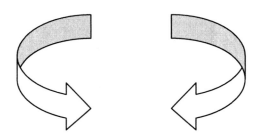

"THE CHURCH"
{AN END TO A MEANS}

It's Practical. It's Biblical. It Works.

<u>THE OUTREACH</u>
(A Means To An End)

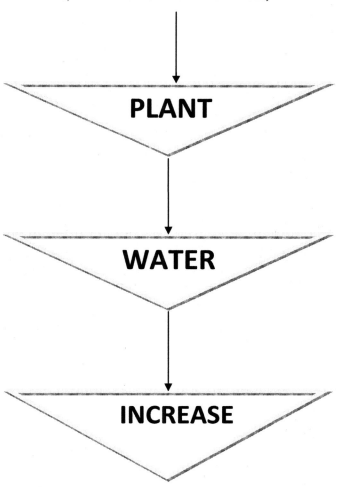

PLANT

WATER

INCREASE

The method in soul winning is to go "out" and "reach" lost souls. Teaching a person to lead requires divine tenets that transform and prepare one for battle. A spiritual soldier should not go out to battle unless God has given him power and proper training with His weaponry. A Christian's weapon is the Word of God, which equips him to destroy, defeat, demolish, disengage, disorient, detect, and devour the enemy. Outreach ministry wins lost souls to Christ and the Church keeps souls rooted in Christ. The Outreach and The Church are practical, biblical, and workable solutions for remediation of Church Inbreed.

I Corinthian 3:6-8 says, "I have planted, Apollos watered; but God gave the increase. (7) So then neither is he that planteth anything, neither he that watereth; but God that giveth the increase. (8) Now he that planteth and he that watereth are one: and every man shall receive his own reward according to his own labor". Man must remember that outreach is purely labor to God. It must maintain biblical doctrine to be effective, infective, and productive. Implementation of effective outreach ministry requires planting and watering. Both tasked with the responsibility to build Gods' Kingdom through the winning of lost souls. These roles function differently and independently for The Outreach and The Church.

Unaware of its importance, Spiritual Leaders who compare planting and watering with harvesting do themselves an injustice. There is no comparison of soul winning with the cultivating and seeding of the heart. Both serve as a means to Salvation and are ordained for the Master's use. Just as important as planting is; so is watering. The watering of the Word of God brings into existence roots that lead to the Salvation of souls; that would otherwise be lost. By no means can servants chaotically perform gratifying outreach ministry being competitive, envy, or jealous. Planting and watering is part of the plan of God in establishing the incorruptible seed in the heart of man for everlasting life through the teaching and preaching of the Gospel. The Outreach methodically descends in the earth from planting, to watering, and Gods' increasing as "A Means to an End". The way Paul, the Apostle, delivered the Word of God to lost souls was by planting seeds of devotion and fidelity to his listeners. The Spirit of God inspired Paul to write his

Epistles as a means to plant His everlasting Word in the lives of all that believed, whether Jew or Greek.

Paul knew his purpose and had no need to compete with the disciples to promote his "Planting Ministry" for self-gain and recognition. His focus was God-driven and God-centered. He planted God's Word in scripture and in the hearts of men so that this heavenly manna could remain forever. He proceeds with scripture stating that Apollos watered. This water is associated with a well of everlasting life that continuously hydrates the soul to maintain a correct spiritual balance. The "Watering Ministry" assigned to Apollos was just as significant as Paul's' Planting Ministry in the development of winning souls to Christ. As important as one may think his ministry is; neither the planting nor watering is effective if God does not give the increase. This affirms that in The Outreach, nothing grows, takes root, or lives unless God increases it. If the planting and watering lack love, the labor is in vain.

The description of planting and watering illustrates Christians being in harmony with the Spirit of Christ. It is a nonproductive Outreach to plant the seed (Word of God) and fail to provide water to nourish it; the crop (Church) suffers and becomes dried out. The spiritual impact of the planting and watering of an outreach ministry affects the maturity and growth of the crop. As evident in scripture, planting and watering are worthless if God does not increase. When the crop (Church) suffers from a lack of spiritual nourishment, the act of worship begins to malfunction. The function of "Outreach" is to perform as a church without walls operating in the world and the "Church" is to continue serving as an organism with walls operating against the world. To be effective, both must operate according to the grace of God. To survive outreach ministry and church leadership, one must be faithfully committed to God and equipped with the Holy Spirit.

Outreach delivers the lost soul to the Church for nourishment and development in the faith. At the inception of conversion, the soul is a new babe in Christ, which is a suitable time to build upon this foundation. I Corinthian 3:10-11 states: "According to the grace of God which is given unto me, as a wise masterbuilder, I have laid the foundation, and another buildeth thereon. But let every man take heed how he buildeth thereupon. (11) For other foundation can no man lay than that is laid, which is Jesus Christ".

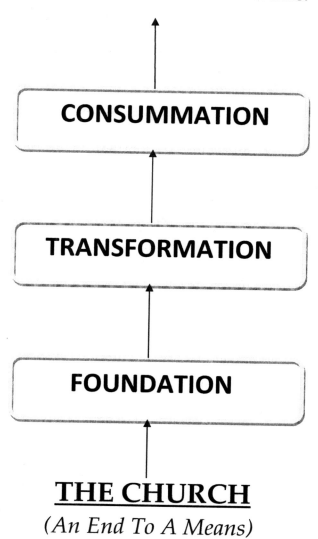

CONSUMMATION

TRANSFORMATION

FOUNDATION

THE CHURCH
(An End To A Means)

The first and most important, but unnoticed part of a building is the foundation. Building upon a Christian foundation demands obedient and holy   servants. Jesus is the foundation that prohibits Church Inbreed and keeps the church from dating the world. Souls built on anything other than the Word of God will perish and live a defeated, vain, and pretentious Christian life. The seed planted and watered during outreach ministry establishes the foundation.   When a soul is born again, not of corruptible seed, but of incorruptible, by the Word of God, he has a confident foundation.

The incorruptible seed planted during outreach and in the preaching and teaching of the Gospel is necessary as *An End to a Means* with salvation in Jesus Christ. A corrupt seed is morally debased and has foreign admixtures that produce Church Inbreed. A corrupt seed manifests the works of the flesh and its' concoction includes attitudes built upon envy, strife, lying, heresies, jealousy, hatred and other complex mixtures that rob Salvation. To put an end to this senseless hybridizing of the church and world, Christians must live in the Spirit as well as walk in Him. This overpowering world movement of Church Inbreed derives from self-indulgence and self-gratification. Born Again Christians cannot live simultaneously as the world and as Christians too. The believer must love the one and hate the other. Matthew 6:24 states: "No man can serve two masters; for either he will hate the one, and love the other, or else he will hold to the one, and despise the other. Ye cannot serve God and mammon".

A man's Salvation ought to motivate him to love others and not lust after things concerning the flesh and the world. Lust is an inordinate desire that traps the believer and lures him away from Christ. The world lusts but the church loves. A combination of love and lust is Church Inbreed, which is an indication of spiritual defection. If this immoral behavior persists, the church will become effete in winning souls to Christ. Furthermore, interbreeding spiritual things with worldly is not the works of Christ but of Satan.

Satan has permeated his principles and ideas among Christians that build upon their foundation with wood, hay, and stubble. A corrective action to remedy Church Inbreed is to flee from fornication, idolatry, and sin. Born Again Christians must build upon the foundation that Christ lay with gold, silver, and precious stones. Since Christ will destroy the world with fire, Christians must use flame-retardant materials that fire will not destroy. The church must build up a spiritual house, a holy temple to offer up spiritual sacrifices, acceptable to God by Jesus Christ. To refrain from Church Inbreed, one must abstain from fleshly lusts that war against the Spirit.

A second way for the remediation of Church Inbreed is the practice of humility. The removal of pride is vital and not an option when one claims Salvation in Jesus Christ. This is essential because God expects every born again believer to cast down imaginations and high things that exalt itself against the knowledge of Him. In order for The Church to overcome *"An End to a Means"*, it requires a transformation of the believer. Romans 12:1-2 states, "I beseech you therefore, brethren, by the mercies of God, that ye present your bodies a living sacrifice, holy, acceptable unto God, which is your reasonable service. (2) And be not conformed to this world: but be ye transformed by the renewing of your mind, that ye may prove what is that good, and acceptable, and perfect, will of God". Breaking free from Church Inbreed is not a matter of downsizing the church, but assuring that Christians are rooted and grounded in the Word of God.

More and more Christians struggle with their faith due to a non-transformed mind and conformity to the world. When the believer is conformed to the world, he has an overindulgence of self, an acceptability of sin, and a superficial abiding of the Law. This act portrayed by Inbred Christians becomes subtle, discreet, and deceptive. What a tragedy! There is a danger in sinning willfully and successfully without convictions. Inbred Christians will continue to struggle with their faith until churches return and become refuges of hope; temples of deliverances; and tabernacles of revivals.

As Born Again Christians, God demands holy and acceptable living sacrifices, which are the lives of the believers. In no way can Christians offer up sacrifices tainted with the world and expect God to receive it. The responsibility of every believer is to be a servant of the Lord and offer as a sacrifice a life devoted to building His Kingdom. This is impossible to do when the mind is not renewed or transformed from the things and love of this world. Transformation comes about when man accepts

Jesus in his heart and chooses to live after the Spirit instead of things in the world. The steps a Christian take to avoid being conformed to the world is that (1) He must receive his new creation in Christ; (2) He must reawaken to the knowledge of Christ; and (3) He must renew his mind from the old man to Christ. This is not a "fly-by-night" process but a discipline involving praying, studying, reading, meditating, and the practice of the Word of God.

One of the most critical birth defects of a born again child of God is mastering the ability to think as Christ. No matter how hard the mind tries to deplete, delete, and depart from things concerning the old man, it unintentionally goes back there. The mind acts magnetically and pulls hidden thoughts that are unholy, conquering, and suggestively enticing. This birth defect somehow leaves the Born Again Christian vulnerable which then open doors for spiritual defeat. Instead of being victorious over the enemy, he/she becomes the victim. As diminutive as it may seem, this birth defect leads to other spiritual handicaps that are crippling, deforming, and imprisoning. Repeatedly, this born again believer succumbs to this unremitting behavior, which frustrates his faith. Eventually, he realizes this recurring mental breakdown, repents, and goes back to the thoughts and ways of Christ. This on-going relapse usually occurs with the Born Again Christian causing a warring in his soul. Nevertheless, since the soul is anchored in Jesus, the results are a transformed mind.

The transformation process focuses on the Born Again Christian building upon a foundation laid in Jesus Christ. This mode of reaching *An End to a Means* is through the act of denying self and being obedient to Christ until death. The mastery of the obedience to Christ comes when Christians know what the promises of God are for their lives. Revelation of the promises of God is open to those who study and read God's Word constantly and refer to the Scriptures as a daily guide for living. It is also necessary to read the Bible to understand the will of God as transformed vessels. Transformed lives produce renewed minds that think on things that are true, honest, just, pure, lovely and are of a good report. This process is essential if the Born Again Christian is to live a victorious life in Jesus.

Oftentimes, defeat overtakes the believer not so much in what he does but in how he thinks and believes. When the transformed man thinks with the old mind, the results are that of the old nature. If he repeatedly experience defeat and witness no progress towards his newfound faith, he assumes God does not acknowledge him and slides back into the world. He finds himself still loving the world and trying to please the Lord; possessing the life of an Inbred Christian.

The reason Inbred Christians sow into the flesh is a lack of discipline and change of mind. Most Christians have a difficult time confessing and acknowledging sin in their lives. Very few people will admit that demoniac influence affect their lives; increasing their sexual appetites; supporting their lying tongues; feeding their manipulative minds; lacing their envying hearts; and substantiating their un-forgiveness. To admit these un-Christ-like characteristics, the Christian must be transparent. A transparent Christian is confident in the faith and has an unwavering trust in the Lord with a great expectancy of hope. The Scripture reads in James 4:7, "Submit yourselves therefore to God. Resist the devil, and he will flee from you". The only way a person can resist the devil is to submit to God. This strengthens the Christian and provides him the fortitude to endure temptations. The problem most Christians face with the devil fleeing them is that they do not recognize him as a threat and do not take him seriously in warfare. Therefore, they find themselves yielding and committing sin frequently. When a person is in denial of sins' existence, he does not seek deliverance through the Word of God but in his own strength. This type of attitude stems from pride and holds the believer hostage against his own will.

An example of resisting the devil is to recognize a particular sin or temptation that surfaces at specific times or at random depending upon circumstances and surroundings. Take notice that these temptations are familiar and stronger than first encountered. Yielding to temptation is sin and this comes from the lack of resistance. Once yielded, the sin becomes familiar and the devil uses this particular sin through and with others to entangle the Christian. A person trapped in a "familiar sin" has a tremendous battle with resistance because the familiar demon is skilled in creating situations that feed the sin. To overcome this influence of the devil, one must submit to God because power is in His Spirit and not the flesh.

The third way to remedy Church Inbreed is through a transformed mind. The transformation process for Salvation is the renewing of the mind, which requires practice; discipline of the flesh; and the replacement of old mindsets with godly wisdom. This kind of wisdom that comes from God: renews the mind, changes the mind, and guards the mind. As the renewed mind becomes as the mind of Christ, the Born Again Christian proceeds to live an abundant, fruitful life. He then positions himself for the consummation of eternal life. The leading of the Holy Spirit promotes godly living in an excellent way. *A Means to an End* outlined in the Outreach Ministry for soul Salvation requires seeding, weeding, and feeding. By way of the Holy Spirit, an incorruptible seed takes root in the heart. After which the Holy Spirit's power roots up any weed previously grown in the heart of man. Then, the Outreach Ministry feeds the soul the engrafted Word of God. This process requires sound, biblical doctrine that generates clean hands and pure hearts. These Christians, who are pure in heart, await Christ's coming not by living haphazardly in sin and as inbreeds, but through watching and praying without ceasing.

Contrariwise, An End to a Means for eternal life is obeying the Word of God, denying self-gratification, and relying totally on Jesus Christ. I Samuel 15:22 states: "Behold, to obey is better than sacrifice, and to hearken than the fat of rams". To obey is to submit willfully to the leading of the Spirit and trust God with all of life's consequences. This obedience overflows to a mindset that pleases God instead of fulfilling the flesh. Denying self-gratification reflects a Christian who has the persistence and stamina to be different and devoted to the mission of Christ. He is often lonely even when he is not alone. When one is lonely, only God can fill the emptiness through the meditation and revelation of His Word. Being alone is quite different from being lonely, which can be satisfied with people, places, or things. The Born Again Christian that obeys God and denies self usually has an extraordinary ability to rely on God's promises. Regardless to circumstantial evidence, the Christian that relies on God will be ready to receive Him when He returns.

I Peter 1: 13, "Wherefore gird up the loins of your mind, be sober, and hope to the end for the grace that is to be brought unto you at the revelation of Jesus Christ". The outcome for the end of the life of the believer is to live out this amazing grace and wait for the Lords' appearing. In the second return of Christ, He plans to present the Born Again Christian as a glorious and holy church, without spot, wrinkle, or blemish. The removal of the curse that brought disobedience into the world will no longer be present. The consummation will separate the godly from the ungodly or better still, the Inbred Christian from the Born Again Christian. In Revelation 22, "And he saith unto me, Seal not the sayings of the prophecy of this book: for the time is at hand. He that is unjust, let him be unjust still: and he which is filthy, let him be filthy still: and he that is righteous, let him be righteous still: and he that is holy, let him be holy still".